52 Psalms in a Year
A Weekly Prayer Companion

By: Israel Jacobs

This book is dedicated to all those who need a little spiritual help throughout the year.

Table of Contents

Forward	pg. i
Week 1	1
Week 2	4
Week 3	7
Week 4	10
Week 5	13
Week 6	16
Week 7	18
Week 8	21
Week 9	24
Week 10	27
Week 11	29
Week 12	31
Week 13	34
Week 14	37
Week 15	39
Week 16	43
Week 17	46
Week 18	49
Week 19	52
Week 20	55
Week 21	57
Week 22	60

Week 23	63
Week 24	65
Week 25	68
Week 26	70
Week 27	72
Week 28	75
Week 29	78
Week 30	80
Week 31	82
Week 32	85
Week 33	88
Week 34	91
Week 35	93
Week 36	97
Week 37	100
Week 38	102
Week 39	105
Week 40	108
Week 41	111
Week 42	113
Week 43	115
Week 44	118
Week 45	121
Week 46	124
Week 47	126
Week 48	129
Week 49	132
Week 50	135

Week 51	138
Week 52	140
Resources	145

Forward

Dear beloved brothers and sisters in Christ –

Yes, beloved! What emotions does my calling you such stir within you? Does it surprise you? Does is shock you to hear me call you such a name? Does such a word make you feel ashamed, saddened, or unworthy?

My dear brothers and sisters, rejoice! For such human emotions are only felt in the presence of total, complete, and overwhelming love. A love that comes directly from He who made all things; this includes you. And, what's more, you were created to be a direct object of that great love! For God needs no mortal comforts to sustain Him; no food, or drink, or rest, or company outside of the Trinity (for the Trinity has been since the Beginning). He needed neither our help in placing the stars in the sky, nor setting the planets in their orbits. Heaven, His abode, was completed before the foundation of the universe. So, for what purpose could humanity have been completed?

Why was Adam called from the dust, life breathed in to him by God? Why was Eve pulled from Adam's rib? Amen, I tell you, the truth is found when we behold the cross! There, the truth of our destiny is revealed in the Truth that is Christ. For love, we were made; made in the image of our Creator. We – saint and sinner, free and slave, every person of every nation – are called to live in a perfect relationship with God. And not perfect because of anything we do on our part. Certainly not! For we are imperfect beings and can only love imperfectly. But perfect because God, who loves us unconditionally, is also perfect, and so, He loves us perfectly. And this love is found on the cross, where Christ – the only begotten Son of God – gave his life so perfectly for us, so that we may be redeemed.

So, yes, I call you beloved! For that is the ultimate truth of what you are. Your truest identity is found in the sacrifice of Christ on the cross. You are a beloved child of the living God. This truth has been written for all in the Gospels, and proclaimed throughout the world for centuries.

So, what is the purpose of the book you now hold in your hands? I write to you to give you strength. As glorious as the truth is, it is often eclipsed by our daily lives. I know this, for I was once like you are now. In fact, I was worse, and consider myself, still, a sinner among sinners, though I am blessed to be writing in the name of God for your benefit. But truly, I tell you, I was once entirely lost in this world; a slave to all that it provided. Every meager distraction that blinded me to the truth.

But no more! I have been called to bring the news of God's great love to you. I write to remind you that you *are* beloved. I write to reveal to you that others have shared and understand your struggles. I write to reaffirm what is already written in the Good News: there is a God who sees your struggles, and will come to you if you but call out to Him. I have provided for you a selection of psalms and my own reflections on these writings. The reflections I give are done to highlight what I deem to be the most important ideas present in the selection from the Book of Psalms. However, do not just take my own insight as all that can be gleaned from the verses. I have also provided for you, after each of my reflections, a place to write your own ideas as you meditate on the psalm for the week.

May the psalms in this book provide you with comfort, insight, encouragement, and above all, peace. May it, as a weekly devotional, be a place to start if you are unsure of how to approach God with your needs, pains, or fears. I write all these things in the name of Christ, the King, whose peace I send to all of you. You, who are beloved!

Your Brother in the Faith,

Israel

52 Psalms in a Year

Week 1

*Blessed is the man who does
not walk in the counsel of the wicked.
Nor stand in the way of sinners,
nor sit in the company with scoffers.
Rather, the law of the LORD is his joy;
and on His law he meditates day and night.*

Psalms 1: 1-2

Week 1 Reflection

What a wonderful set of words! I thought it fitting, when writing this book, that the first week's psalm should be Psalm 1. The psalm has one simple, encouraging message: that we should follow God's word and keep His commandments. We should, as the Christian faithful, avoid "the company of scoffers." For how can we say we truly follow God if the company of our choice is comprised of those who would openly mock or insult the Almighty? Does that not reflect poorly on our faith? The psalm also advises us not to "stand in the way of sinners." In doing this, we avoid imitating behavior we know to be against our beliefs. Instead, we are to look to God and his law for insight into which path is the right path, and the strength to walk it.

But do not think the psalmist meant for such life changing decisions to be made on a whim. And do not think that following the law of God to be something you will easily fall into the routine of doing. That is why the psalmist also advises us to meditate on the Lord's law "day and night." We are reminded in these few words that becoming better followers of the Word is a daily, nightly, and yes, even lifelong process.

This is also not just advice for the words of the Bible, or the words of the Book of Psalms. It is advice that I would recommend you carry for this book as well. Yes, you are free to read it at your leisure. I certainly can't stop you from reading the entire thing in a week, or even less! However, I encourage you to take it slow. Listen to the words of Psalm 1. Try taking things one week at a time, as was the intention of the writer. Read both the psalm and the reflection, and meditate on it, day and night. Bring yourselves to truly comprehend both my words, and the words of the psalms. Use the entirety of the week to reflect on what these words mean to you, and what truth they may hold for your life.

Weekly Thoughts

Week 2

*Know that the LORD works wonders for His faithful one;
the LORD hears when I call out to Him.*

Psalms 4:4

Week 2 Reflection

I'd like to start off this week's reflection by posing to you a simple (although, you may also think it strange) question. The question is this: how good is your hearing? If someone calls your name, do you hear it clearly? How far away can a person stand and you still be able to make out what they said? Are you a good eavesdropper? Are you able to hear even that which is said at no more than a whisper? If someone shouts to you at a great distance, is it just a loud noise, or can you still interpret the sound as words?

Hopefully, you have a good set of ears. Though I myself may have lost the genetic lottery when it comes to my eyesight, I feel that my hearing is fairly good. But even the person with the most miraculous pair of ears in the world, who can manage feats of extraordinary hearing well beyond that of normal, cannot accomplish what God can with His sense of listening. To prove it, let me ask a different set of questions.

Pick anyone near you, if indeed you are near others. What are they thinking? Can you hear their thoughts? What's rattling around inside that head of theirs? If you are alone, I want you to imagine someone you know very well, no matter where they are in the world at the moment. Can you hear them? Whether across the street and in their house, or across the country and the same, are you able to hear them? Now imagine a criminal. Imagine someone alone in a cell.

Imagine one who is homeless, out on the streets or in a shelter. Can you hear them? What are *their* thoughts? Can you hear that with your ears? If you are like me, the answer is 'no.'

But God hears. Who but God can hear all these? Who but God can know our inner thoughts? Who but God can hear the cries of our hearts? The psalm this week reminds us of Gods great hearing. When we call out to Him, no matter where we are, He hears us. He hears from Heaven the tear drops of those who grieve. He hears through the stone walls of a cell, the repentance of a sinner. He hears the simple longings of those who go hungry. God hears the cries of His children. Not a single one goes unheard. And, just as God *hears*, He also *does*.

The psalmist tells us to "know that the Lord works wonders for His faithful one." So, not only should we give thanks that God is never too far away to hear our honest prayers to Him, but also that He – according to His wisdom – will "work wonders" in our lives. To God, how long we've been away, how long it has taken to cry out to Him, is of no concern. So, call out to God. He is listening.

Weekly Thoughts

Week 3

*The LORD has heard my plea;
the Lord will receive my prayer.*

Psalms 6:9-10

Week 3 Reflection

For this week, I would like to draw your attention to the second part of the psalmist's prayer. Last week, we spoke together of God's great ability to hear. Of how, no matter where we are, or what we've done, or how long it has been since we dropped a line, we are never too far away for God; He hears us always. Now, let us look at the word "receive", found in this week's psalm. It is an interesting choice for the psalmist.

Usually when we use the word "receive", we speak of an occasion when we were given a gift of some kind. Rarely do we "receive" something bad. For, to truly receive anything, we must take whatever it is. We must be willing, and if we are willing, we are therefore, usually, glad to get whatever has been delivered to us. We receive birthday gifts. We receive good news. We receive a visit from an old friend or family member. When the thing being delivered is negative, we tend to use a different word. We say we "get", meaning we were not happy to be delivered this thing, and, had it been up to us, we would not been given whatever it was at all. We get bad news. We get fired from our jobs. We get scolded or reprimanded.

Bearing this in mind, let us now turn our attention to the psalm. It does not say that, when we pray to God, He will "get my prayer." Rather, the psalmist made a point to say, "The Lord will receive my prayer." This means that, not only is God *always* listening to our prayers, but, even more miraculously, He is *happy* to hear from us! Keep this in mind the next time you think you may not be important enough for God to hear you calling out to Him. He is a loving God, attentive to our needs, and He will *always* be delighted to hear from you.

Weekly Thoughts

Week 4

*When I see your heavens, the work of your fingers,
the moon and stars that you set in place –
what is man that you are mindful of him, and a son
of man that you care for him? You have made him a
little less than a god [the angels] and crowned him
in glory and honor.*

Psalms 8:4-6

Week 4 Reflection

At some point this week, when it is dark outside, I want you to go out and look up at the night sky. Make sure it's a clear night, with little to no clouds. I want you to be able to see as many stars as you can. If you want, or are able to, take along some binoculars or even a telescope. Gaze into the sky, as so many have done before you. And, like those who contemplated the heavens, contemplate this week's psalm.

A long time ago – nearly 4000 years in fact – Abraham, the Patriarch, was outside his tent on a similar night. God spoke to him, telling him to, "Look up at the sky and count the stars, if you can." (Gn.15:4) Quite the task on Abraham's part. Modern day space technology has calculated that there is around one septillion (that's a one followed by 24 zeros!) stars in the observable universe. But God was not interested in Abraham's ability to count; He was interested in his faith. Among all these stars, not a single one is the same. Each is unique, as are the planets that orbit them. And, though they are far away and appear as mere twinkling lights, the moon is much closer; it appears as a great, beautiful orb, lighting our night.

Behold all this beauty! Behold all of these things that overwhelm us with their perfect design and adherence to the laws of nature. Gaze at the night sky and behold the absolute perfection of the universe in motion. Now, consider this: the same God who set the universe spinning – designing it perfectly, down to the smallest detail – considers all these lesser in beauty to you. Stars, suns, moons, planets, and the things they contain, all pale in comparison in the eyes of our Lord to His greatest creation: humanity.

Though we were created with less power and strength, the psalmist reminds us that we were, in fact, created in importance *above* angels. The angels themselves are instructed to help humanity in our struggles, according to the will of God. Take some time this week to consider how loved you are. So loved, that the whole of Creation does not receive as much care and attention as a single human being. When you go star gazing, let the beauty of the night and all it contains remind you of the great love God has for you. Like Abraham, see the stars and have faith that God will provide for your wellbeing. You are ever at the forefront of His mind; your care is His primary concern.

> *I can see how it might be possible for a man to*
> *look down upon the earth and be an atheist,*
> *but I cannot conceive how a man could look up*
> *into the heavens and say there is no God.*
>
> *- Abraham Lincoln*

Weekly Thoughts

Week 5

The LORD rules forever,
has set up His throne for judgement.
It is He who judges the world with justice,
who judges the peoples with fairness.
The LORD is a stronghold for the oppressed,
a stronghold in times of trouble.

Psalms 9:8-10

Week 5 Reflection

This week, let us talk about two new (and often unheard of) views of God, offered to us by the psalmist. *God as Judge*, and *God as Stronghold*. We will start with the easier of the two to wrap our minds around; the one we are the most familiar with. Its familiarity may come from the fact that it is the one we talk about the most or hear about the most in our church communities. Let us look at *God as Stronghold*.

Describing the Creator as a stronghold is a fairly easy concept to grasp. Much like any stronghold, He is strong, mighty, sturdy, and a place of refuge. In Him, as in any secure dwelling, we find rest. Rest from our fears; rest from our worries; rest from our enemies. A respite from all that ails us can be found here, in the arms of our Heavenly Father. In Him, we take refuge from the storm of our lives. We can rely on Him because none is above Him. Scripture tells us that all good things come from the Lord, so we rest in that knowledge. We have faith that, when the storm rages, our mighty fortress will hold steady.

Now, let us look at the other image of God described in the psalm. We, as human beings, have a tendency to not consider God as the Judge as often or as thoroughly as we should. It is, for lack of a better word, an uncomfortable way for us to view the Lord. In our minds, it comes into conflict with the image we have of a benevolent Creator and loving Father. But as you read of "God the Judge" in this week's psalm, I encourage you to be at peace. Your worries exist only as a result of your – and many others, including my own at one point – human standard of fairness and judgement.

No human judge will ever be like God, who is *the* Judge. Not even those who sit on the Supreme Court, the highest court in my homeland, will ever judge with such fairness, wisdom, and righteousness as is known only to the Lord. How wonderful it is, then, that we humans are not the final say in cases of salvation. It is necessary, in the world of men, to have a system of human laws that orders and governs our societies. And it is also necessary to elect those to be guardians of said laws, and see to it that they are adhered to. But even those we entrust with such duties can fail us.

Ask yourselves this: would you trust any mortal man to judge you fairly at the time of your death? Would you leave it up to any single human being to decide where your immortal soul will spend eternity, when one said destination is hell? If your answer is, "No," then again, I encourage you to be at peace. Take comfort that there is one, and only one, who judges with absolute fairness. One that will make sure that those who do good will be repaid with good; those who do evil repaid with evil. And not according to our limited understanding of justice, but according to His perfect justice. Even redemption itself is based on God's ability to judge correctly. For it was God who judged the world as needing of salvation. It was God who judged the best way possible to carry out that salvation. It was God who judged the human race, despite our grievous sins, as being worthy of redeeming. When we think of God as a judge in the light of a human court, we are afraid. But, if we instead think of God as a judge in the light of the cross, we will be comforted.

You judge your children worthy of love…
Now you know Papa's heart.

- Wisdom (The Shack, 2017)

Weekly Thoughts

Week 6

*But I trust in Your mercy. Grant my heart joy
in your salvation, I will sing to the LORD,
for He has dealt bountifully with me!*

Psalms 13:6

Week 6 Reflection

In a world that seems quite happy to kick us around, the idea of God's mercy can seem foreign to us. We might often feel as though His mercy is far away, or even non-existent. But do not be too hasty to lay such blame on God. Consider the psalmist's choice of words for this week. King David (the author of this psalm and many others) says that he "trusts" in the Lord's mercy. He asks humbly that God, "Grant my heart joy…." We gather from this that David is in the process of praying for mercy to be delivered to him, not that he has already received it. He trusts that God will hear his prayer, and reflects on the other times he has been rescued by God's grace.

David exclaims that he "will sing to the Lord" when he is reminded of all the times in his life that he has called upon God and been answered. He can count them all, every instance, and takes comfort in their number. He sings because the Lord has shown such great kindness; "He has dealt bountifully with me!" Now, it is your turn. Look back on your own life and see the times when God has come to you. Look back and see His mercy at work in your life. Know that God does not grant mercy because we want it, or even deserve it. He grants mercy because He is happy to give it. All you must do is trust.

Weekly Thoughts

Week 7

*The fool says in his heart,
"There is no God."*

Psalms 14:1

Week 7 Reflection

There is more evidence for the miracle of the Resurrection of Christ than for nearly every other ancient historical event. If Christ was raised, then all he preached must have been true, for by his Resurrection he proved he was, in fact, the Son of God. Therefore, the existence of such a God must also be a reality. This also means that the primary truths of the Genesis story of Creation are valid. Those being: this universe was created; Creation was perfect in its design; humanity was created to be in a relationship with God; humanity sinned, and Creation was made imperfect; what follows after the Fall is the story of God's redemption of the human race.

So why, then, are there those that still deny the existence of God? Why, then, are there "fools" who say in their hearts, "There is no God?" If there is such evidence, then to deny God *is* foolishness. The reason is simple: such people are afraid of the light this perspective shines on their lives. For, as there is the reality of God's redemption, there is also the reality that we need such redemption. To accept the existence of God is to accept the reality of sin, and the consequences that follow. Truly, it is easier to commit all number of atrocities if there exists no higher authority to judge us.

But, dear brothers and sisters, while this reasoning is born out of ignorance or pride, it is perpetuated by fear. Fear of the eternal consequence of sin not forgiven, yes, but also of such forgiveness itself. Those who commit sin fear the pain of being truly known by a loving God, who has forgiven their sins. A God who, when presented with the choice of suffering death or letting us be forever separated from Him, chose the former. So, it is easier to pretend that such a God doesn't exist, rather than go through the pain of admitting our own faults, laying them before the cross, and being embraced by Christ's loving redemption.

So, be strong my brothers and sisters. Resist such foolishness. But more so than yourselves, help others to give up their own foolishness. Help them to overcome their fears of judgement, and realize the truth of God's peace and forgiveness. For he who dies a fool, is a fool forever. But he who dies in Christ, will have life everlasting.

Weekly Thoughts

Week 8

*You have tried me by fire, but found no malice in me.
My mouth has not transgressed as others do.
As Your lips have instructed me, I have kept from the
way of lawlessness. My steps have kept to Your paths;
my feet have not faltered.*

Psalms 17:3-5

Week 8 Reflection

The majority of this psalm is easy to comprehend. We are willing to apply all that the psalmist exalts of himself to our own lives. We, the faithful of Christ, say to ourselves, "Surely I have kept from lawlessness," or, "Surely my feet have not faltered." But let us not be too hasty in this self-congratulation. When was the last time, by your reckoning, you were tested by fire? And I do not mean for you to recall a meager inconvenience; something trivial, passing quickly and easily forgotten until now. I ask you, when was the last time you faced a raging inferno, rather than a tiny blaze? I realize such traumatic experiences are unpleasant to recall, but I ask you to pray for God's strength and remember the trial. Now, through all that happened, can you honestly say you did not falter? Did you truly keep to God's path?

Did you truly remain faithful to all that God commanded you during this difficult time? Did you condemn someone with your words? Then your "mouth has… transgressed", for God calls us to forgive even our enemies. Did you feel He abandoned you? God says that we are never alone. Did you blame the Lord for your troubles? Then you have not "kept from the way of lawlessness", for it is written that all good comes from God. All evil is the workings of the devil.

    Will you lie now, and say that none of these things has ever come to pass? That you never blamed God, or felt anger towards him? We often forget how easy it is to have strength in our faith when times are good. But when our trials come – and they will come – does this strength remain? When we are tested, that is when God will ask us if we still love Him. He will ask us if we still have faith in His works, and that He will lead us out of the fire. When Daniel's friends were tossed into the furnace for not worshipping the idol of King Nebuchadnezzar, they went in still rejoicing in the Lord. For their faith, God led them out again, unharmed. We must trust that God will do the same when our trials come. That, when the flames rise high around us, we will be safe from the heat.

Weekly Thoughts

Week 9

*The law of the LORD is perfect,
refreshing to the soul.
The decree of the LORD is trustworthy,
giving wisdom to the simple...
The command of the LORD is clear,
enlightening the eye.*

Psalms 19:8,9

Week 9 Reflection

Similar to what we spoke about on Week 5, the psalmist writes to us this time of God's law, decrees, and commands. We are told that when we reflect on all these, we are granted certain gifts as a result. We are told that the law is "refreshing to the soul." The decrees are described as "trustworthy", and they give wisdom to those who are not wise. The commands that come from God are clear, and said to be "enlightening to the eye."

God gives all three aspects of his Justice – law, decrees, and commands – freely to His people. His Law is the Ten Commandments, given to Moses and the ancient Hebrew nation. His decrees are the wisdom He gives to those called to special positions in the world, such as priests, saints, or even those with special talents who are called to put those talents in His service. His commands are only two: love God with all your heart, soul, mind, and strength, and love your neighbor as yourself. He gives all these things, but allows us to choose whether to follow them or not.

Our ability to choose is an act of God's love for humanity. For no father would force his children to love him. So, how much more would our Heavenly Father refuse to force all of us here to love Him? Even if our disobedience – as being a part of that choice – causes Him pain. But He isn't the only one who is hurt. If we choose to ignore that which refreshes the soul, our soul is in rotten health. It can no longer feel or hear the Lord. All spiritual, and even some physical, problems stem from a rotten spirit. If we choose to not accept God's decrees, decrees we know to be trustworthy, we deny ourselves wisdom, and thus, remain simple minded. If we choose to ignore His commands, the two greatest commands, to love Him and our neighbor, then we are blinded to the truth.

Spiritual refreshment, wisdom, and true sight, are all gifts given by the Lord. His law, decrees, and commands, are all worthy of your absolute and total trust. So, put your faith in Him. Let him work wonders in your life. Let your soul and body be healed. These, and other gifts, await all those who have faith in God.

Weekly Thoughts

Week 10

Yet You are enthroned as the Holy One;
You are the glory of Israel.
In You our fathers trusted;
they trusted and You rescued them.
To You they cried out and escaped;
in You they trusted and were not disappointed.

Psalms 22:4-6

Week 10 Reflection

My advice for you this week, my brothers and sisters, is the same as the psalmist's. In times of distress, cry out to the Lord. Let your pain come, your heart ache, and your eyes be filled with tears. But, in doing all this, do not let your spirit be troubled. Bring all your pain to the Lord. Lay it all down at the foot of the cross. God is on His throne; He is the "Holy One… the glory of Israel." As your forefathers in the faith trusted in His power to save, so you should trust all the same. You have cause to trust even more, for so many of God's good deeds – proof of His saving power – have been written down and spoken about for centuries. If you are looking for a way out of a difficult situation, cry out to the Lord. He will hear you. He will trade your ashes for beauty. And the most important thing to remember is this: He *has never* and *will never* disappoint.

Weekly Thoughts

Week 11

*Even though I walk through the
valley of the shadow of death,
I will fear no evil, for You are with me...*

Psalms 23:4

Week 11 Reflection

Recall, dear brothers and sisters, the raging fire I spoke of in Week 8. We ask, plead, beg God that such a blaze never arrives. We wish for nothing but peace in our lives. None of us asks for struggles. But no matter how hard we pray, struggle arrives all the same. The fire comes upon us, and often overwhelms us. So, now that the hard times are here, how will we handle the situation? How will we make sure that our faith remains? For faith in the Lord is the only thing that will keep the inferno from consuming us.

Repeat the words of this psalm, probably one of the most easily recognized and well known of all of the psalms. We are told by the psalmist, King David, that even when we are in the midst of hell, God is never far from us. Even when our enemies close in around us, the Creator is by our side. He is faithful; He is our constant companion. So, go forth, and face your trials. Fear no evil, for the God of the heavens and the earth, is by your side. Even if a great shadow of evil things comes upon you, keep walking forward. With faith, even this great shadow will not prevent you from seeing the true light of God. And it is this light that will lead you out of the valley and on to green pastures.

Weekly Thoughts

Week 12

*Good and upright is the LORD, therefore
He shows sinners the way,
He guides the humble in righteousness,
and teaches the humble His way…
For the sake of Your name, LORD, pardon my guilt,
though it is great.*

Psalms 25:8-9,11

Week 12 Reflection

In a clear example of God's salvation plan, present throughout the story of the Bible, David testifies to the ministry of his descendent – the Messiah, Jesus. He tells us that God, because He is Good (not just good as humans are good, but the progenitor of all that *is* good, thus being Goodness itself) will lead all those who are humble in the way… "His way." This especially goes for sinners, who are the most lost and need the most guidance. The psalmist asks that God pardon his guilt, "even though it is great." David recognizes that God possesses the power to take away the burden of sin, pardoning us for our mistakes. The Hebrew king finishes by saying all this can be accomplished "for the sake of [God's] name."

In the Gospel of John, chapter 14, we see the Apostles gathered together with Christ for the Last Supper. What follows in the ensuing chapters is a long discourse about Jesus' mission on earth, as well as the path the Apostles are to take once Christ has left them. The Apostles are initially confused by their teacher's words. Thomas even asks Jesus how it is possible for any of them to follow Him if they don't know where he is going, and, therefore, don't know the way. Jesus says this in response: "I am the Way, and the

Truth, and the Life." Here, we see the full revelation of David's psalm.

God leads *all* who are humble, to His Son, who is the Way. Through Him, we are guided; we are instructed by following His example. In the name of Christ, miracles are accomplished. In the book after John's Gospel (Acts), we see many of these miracles performed by the early disciples of Christ. Men and women who, by the Romans and Jews, were called "Followers of the Way." It is in the name of Jesus, who is both God and the Son of God, that sin is forgiven. By the sacrifice of the cross, praying in the name of Christ can be the turning point for us, no matter where we are in our lives. By following Him, we sinners can be shown the Way.

Weekly Thoughts

Week 13

*The LORD is my light and my salvation;
of whom should I be afraid?*

Psalms 27A:1

Week 13 Reflection

This psalm should appear familiar to most church-goers. It is often sung as a part of the service, usually as the responsorial, after the first reading from the Bible. However, the words can pop up in some fashion in hymns sung at any point during worship. Adding to its recognition is the simplicity with which it is written, making it easy to remember. Yet, this simple psalm speaks to us about a great truth. Whom should we fear?

Surely, there are many things in life that we can be afraid of. Fear is a natural instinct, one that has served humanity well for countless generations. Even when we recall our earliest memories, memories that should be happy since they were from when we were more carefree – before life had begun to take its toll on us – we can recall being afraid of something. Whether it was monsters in the closet or under the bed; the dark or things outside our window; being lost or away from our parents for too long. And as we grow older, fear does not leave us. We can develop a myriad of different phobias, from heights to enclosed spaces. We have everyday things that cause us to worry and fret. The car, our job, the house, our kids, our education, *their* education. Fear is a part of life.

The psalm does not tell us that we will never *feel* afraid. It doesn't lie to us and say that if we pray, God will take away our fear. Instead, the psalm speaks the truth to us: whom should we fear?

When fear comes, why should we give in to it? Why should we let fear hold us back when God is ready to give us great courage? Courage is not the absence of fear, but the ability to overcome fear itself. That is what God provides. When life throws something at us and says, "Be afraid," God asks us, "Am I not on the throne? Did I not say I would protect you? Did I not show you how loved you are?" Trust in Him; respond, "Yes, I believe you have my best interests in mind." Show fear that it will not rule you, for God rules your heart.

Weekly Thoughts

Week 14

*Hear my voice, LORD, when I call;
have mercy on me and answer me.
"Come," says my heart, "seek His face";
Your face, LORD, do I seek!*

Psalms 27B:7-8

Week 14 Reflection

If it is in your heart to truly do the will of the Lord, then this psalm has the perfect advice for you. Seek His face. Commit fully to learning, understanding, and knowing the Lord. For no effort in regards to coming to God can be done in half measures. But be prepared, for such a change can be life altering. Truly, I tell you, when you commit your soul to following God's will, your heart will begin to cry out for Him. When you put all your effort toward God, loving Him with all your heart, body, mind, and soul, there will be nothing sweeter in this world for you. God will become your greatest joy. Your soul will be set ablaze, and only God will be enough to quench it.

Weekly Thoughts

Week 15

*Do not drag me off with the wicked,
with those who do wrong,
who speak peace to their neighbors,
though evil is in their hearts.
Repay them for their deeds,
for the evil that they do.
For the work of their hands repay them;
give them what they deserve.*

Psalms 28:3-4

Week 15 Reflection

This week's psalm I want to use as a warning for you, brothers and sisters. Please, before you skip this reflection because you are disheartened that it is not entirely hopeful, know that I only do this because wisdom does not always come dressed in the trappings of joy. I do this for your benefit, so that you may grow in knowledge of Christ, and your hearts may seek Him more earnestly.

This week, in Psalm 28, the writer is crying out to the Lord for deliverance. He wishes to be saved from the wicked, and be separated from them in the process. The psalmist asks if God could divide him from the count of wicked, to not count him "with those who do wrong." The psalmist wants God to be make clear distinctions between him and those that are against him and his Lord. But I ask of you, dear brothers and sisters, who are "the wicked?" Who do you say number among their ranks?

Surely, those who kill? Those who spill innocent blood? Those who fill our streets with all manner of narcotics? Those who start wars over some petty disagreement? Those who break any number of the Commandments of God? Surely all of these we can count among the wicked? And, as surely as we number this lot and say in our hearts, "They are condemned," we also look at ourselves and say, "I am not like them. I am saved." But, if you look closely, and read carefully, these are not the "wicked" that the psalmist describes.

Instead, he talks about those who "speak peace to their neighbors, though evil is in their hearts." I doubt those of you reading this book have committed murder, but allow me to pose to you a scenario. One that is common enough; you might have even experienced such an occurrence in your own lives once or twice. Have you ever been driving, have someone cut you off, and you responded by hurling obscenities at them? Have you ever seen someone going too fast on the road and hoped that they would be pulled over? Have you judged someone by what they were wearing, how they talked, or the color of their skin? Now, answer me this: Do you still go to church and claim that you pray for the salvation of all peoples?

My friends, with all love and respect, I must tell you that *you* are the wicked! Of course, I do not cast stones, for I have been numbered among the wicked as well. In fact, I was the most wicked of all; a rotten sinner with a rotten soul. For I claimed to know and preach in the name of God, but all the while I committed shameful acts. But, much like the Apostle Paul, who breathed murderous threats against the church but then came to be one of its greatest defenders – all thanks to the love of God – I, too, have been rescued from the depths of my sin. So, when I say that you are the wicked the psalmist speaks of, it is not done out of condemnation, but out of a desire to open your eyes to the truth and reconcile you to one another and to God.

The psalmist tells us that the wicked will be repaid. Not according to any human concepts of justice, but according to God's eternal and perfect Justice. So, repent of your ill will, if you have any. Do not carry such evil thoughts, for they ruin the heart and degrade the soul. Instead, speak peace and comfort to your brother. Tell of God's condemnation but more so of his forgiveness. Offer forgiveness to others, not harsh words. Take heed and hear the song of David.

Cast out malice, for it is a tool of the Enemy. He will use it to drive a wedge between you and your neighbor. Instead, love your neighbor as you love yourselves. Fill your heart with compassion; the same compassion that was shown to you on the cross. For we are all sinners, yet Christ died for all. So, model your life after His. Then, you will be counted, not among the wicked, but among the righteous.

Weekly Thoughts

Week 16

*I praise You, LORD, for you raise me up
and did not let my enemies rejoice over me.
O LORD, my God, I cried out to You for help
and you healed me...
You changed my morning into dancing;
You took off my sackcloth and clothed me with gladness*

Psalms 30:2-3,12

Week 16 Reflection

I wish to begin this week by posing a question to you, dear readers. A question that I humbly ask you to seriously contemplate in full. The question is this: Can you think of any good father who would wish to see his child suffer? Take a moment to consider all that I am asking. Perhaps you are thinking of your own father in your consideration. Whatever your answer to the question may be, and whatever the successes or failings of our earthly fathers, I know one thing for certain. If I were I to pose the same question to our Heavenly Father, He would respond with a thunderous, "No!"

He, who is the greatest of all our fathers, will do all in His power to rescue us. He will do all that is in His power to pull us through whatever danger we find ourselves in. If we but call on His name, and trust in His mercy, He will come to us in our suffering. The psalmist reminds us of the good that can come from our devotion to God and His saving grace.

We are told that our enemies will not rejoice over us. We will be healed from all that afflicts us. Our mourning will be turned into dancing; our attitudes changed for the better. Our mourning clothes themselves will be swapped with clothes of gladness. Inwardly and outwardly, we will be healed, and all will be able to see. Contrary to popular belief, God does not wish to see us suffer. So, if we but ask for his saving hand to rescue us, we will see a time when our deepest fears and feelings of sadness will be turned to joy.

Weekly Thoughts

Week 17

To all my foes I am a thing of scorn, and especially
to my neighbors, a horror to my friends.
When they see me in public, they quickly turn away.
I am forgotten, out of mind like the dead...
I hear the whispers of the crowd...
But I trust in You, LORD...
My destiny is in Your hands.

Psalms 31:12-13,14,15,16

Week 17 Reflection

My friends, hear the psalmist and take comfort in his words. Hear both his warning and his praise. Yes, even a warning can provide comfort. For a warning well received can be followed. By the change it brings, we can come to know peace. When we stumble in sin, we may look up from the dirt and see that even our "friends" have deserted us. We look around, only to find that we are alone. Those we once held so dear, and considered our closest allies, have now joined the crowd of scoffers. They mock and scorn you, because they themselves have weakness of heart.

But my dearest readers, take heart. Do not let these times overwhelm you. For even if you see all abandoning you, there is one who will never leave your side. Even when you sin, and become a "thing of scorn", God will be ever present. For it is not in God's nature to so quickly condemn. He offers a path to salvation and forgiveness. Even when those who once knew you forget you because of your sin, quick to judge and even quicker to sentence, do not be discouraged. God will never be so easily swayed. He will ignore the cries of those who wish to see your ruin, and instead listen to the cries of your heart.

Weekly Thoughts

Week 18

*Then I declared my sin to You; my guilt I did not hide.
I said, "I confess my transgression to the LORD",
and You took away the guilt of my sin.*

Psalms 32: 5

Week 18 Reflection

"The greatest lie the Devil ever told was convincing the world he doesn't exist". These chilling (but honest) words were spoken by actor Kevin Spacey in the film *The Usual Suspects*. They reflect to us a truth that is often not acknowledged by many, both among the faithful and unfaithful. Though hard to imagine, and even harder to see at times, the battle for the souls of humanity has already been fought and won. The victory of salvation over condemnation; faith over doubt; life over death. This victory is displayed for all to see on the cross. By giving up His life to save ours, Jesus once again opened the way for humanity to enter the Kingdom of Heaven. Sin would no longer prevail against us, and death had lost its sting. We were no longer doomed by the sin of Adam. Instead, we were freed by the sacrifice of Christ.

Yet, there are still many who may never know the eternal peace of God. There are still many who, by their choice, will go down to the Pit. Why? Because they have been deceived by Satan's greatest lie. Though he is not victorious, the devil is still cunning and, certainly, vindictive. If he convinces us that he no longer exists, then, by association, sin must also not exist. If there is no sin, there is no need to be saved. But herein we find the danger of the lie. Sin *does* exist, and so does salvation from sin. But the first step in this salvation is confession. If we go to our deaths without confessing our sins, then we, in essence, say that there is no need to confess for sin doesn't exist. And, if sin doesn't exist, neither does salvation, and if salvation, Heaven.

The psalmist, this week, points us to the first step in our journey of salvation: confession. Christ, through His death, has provided a path to Heaven and to God. However, to begin walking this path, we must first cast off that which tethers us to this world. No runner starts the race with a bag laden with heavy objects. So, Christ asks us also to lay our burdens down, and accept the burden of the cross, for it is much lighter. We must acknowledge our sin, declaring it to the Lord. The devil wants us to be weighed down by our guilt. He wants us to ignore our sins, and thus, ignore Him who takes them away.

I urge you all, dear brothers and sisters, to look within. I know it will be painful. I, too, am a great sinner, and was a greater sinner before. I, too, looked inward and found pain, want, desire, lust, and all manner of wicked things. I found fault and ugliness within myself. But when I brought all these to God, I was reminded of His everlasting grace. I was reminded that, in His eyes, I am not ugly, but beautiful. Do not let the snares of the devil keep you chained to the things of this world. Do not believe his lies, for you are beautiful too. Christ seeks to forgive, so first, you must forgive yourselves. Upon doing this, you will know the peace that only God can provide.

Weekly Thoughts

Week 19

*Give thanks to the LORD on the harp;
on the ten-stringed lyre offer praise.
Sing to Him a new song;
skillfully play with joyful chant.*

Psalms 33:1-3

Week 19 Reflection

One of my favorite movies of all time is *The Legend of Bagger Vance*. It *is* a golf movie, so it may not appeal to all. But I whole heartedly recommend it, even if you aren't a fan of golf or even the sports genre of film in general. It stars Will Smith as the titular character, Matt Damon in the second lead role, and a wonderful cast of supporting characters.

In the film, the narrator is an older version of a character we meet as a young boy, named Hardy. Young Hardy spends the film by the side of Bagger Vance (Smith), who caddies for golf champion Rannulph Junuh (Damon), during a tournament. At one point, reflecting on the first day of play, an older Hardy says to the audience, "They say God is happiest when His children are at play." This sentiment is clearly present in the psalm we just read.

The psalmist, a musician himself, instructs us how to act when we feel overjoyed by God's goodness. When we feel the need to rejoice and give praise to God, we are encouraged to grab all manner of instruments and sing. Indeed, music can be a powerful tool of worship; a magnificent way to glorify the Creator. And as we sing and dance and make merry in His name, so too, will God look down and delight in our merriment. Remember that the book of

Samuel tells us "David and all the house of Israel danced before the Lord…" (2 Sm. 6:5) as the Ark was being transported into Jerusalem.

So, my friends, dance and sing! Give praise to the Lord, who is worthy of all praise! Sing with your voices, play your instruments, and dance in both body and spirit. Let yourselves be caught up by the moment and feel your souls renewed. When you find that you can no longer contain your joy, don't. The Lord loves to hear you make merry in His name. For it is then, that He is happiest.

Weekly Thoughts

Week 20

I will bless the LORD at all times;
His praise shall always be in my mouth.

Psalms 34:2

Week 20 Reflection

Though a rather unfortunate circumstance, it is not uncommon these days to hear all manner of curses, blasphemies, and foul language flow from the mouths of men, women, and even children. In all forms of media – movies, music, television, books, news – it seems that swearing is ever prevalent. While I will not pass judgement, I cannot help but be discouraged by this ever-increasing trend. While not a grievous sin, it is still heartbreaking to see and hear the mouths of so many utter foul words, when the mouth, tongue, throat, and all manner of bodily organs used for speech, were created to give praises to God.

As a means of breaking this habit – a habit I once carried as well – I offer you this week's psalm. The writer comes to us with some clever advice. If you only use your mouth to glorify the Lord, it will be easy to refrain from foul language. I am sure that we have all heard the phrase, "If you don't have something nice to say, better to say nothing at all." This is the lesson I give this week. For this does not just apply to the utterance of mean spirited or hurtful words to others. This also goes for the utterance of obscenities. So, use your mouth for worship, and ask God's help to buck the trend of swearing.

Weekly Thoughts

Week 21

*Surely, I will wait for the LORD;
who bends down to me and hears my cry;
draws me up from the pit of destruction,
out of the muddy clay, sets my feet upon rock,
steadies my steps, and puts a new song in my mouth,
a hymn to our God.*

Psalms 40A:2-4

Week 21 Reflection

I am quite confident that, at some point in our lives, we have all heard the saying, "All good things come to those who wait." It is a common enough phrase, often spoken to impatient children (or adults still in need of a reminder). It's meaning is quite easy to grasp, making it a perfect medium to impart the lesson of patience and the reward for patience. God, more often than we would like, asks of us this very same patience. I was once taught that, when answering our prayers, God will respond in three very distinct ways. He will say, "Yes", "No", or "Wait". And while we are satisfied with the "Yes" and the "No" – though certainly happier with the "Yes" – we are often left agitated by the "Wait". But it is this waiting that God will ask us to do almost all of the time.

In such moments as these, we must remember the lesson of "All good things come to those who wait." God wants good things for us, and, indeed, has good things planned. We tend to miss these by our rushing, presuming to know what is best for our lives and chasing after immediate gratification. All too often, the things we chase after offer only fleeting moments of happiness, or even end up hurting us. We inevitably end up saying, "If only I had waited." For good things *are* promised to you, in reward for your waiting. The psalm this week is a reminder of that. So, wait for the Lord. He will deliver all good things to you, repaying you for your great faith.

Weekly Thoughts

Week 22

*As the deer longs for streams of water,
so, my soul longs for You, O God.
My soul thirsts for God, the living God.*

Psalms 42:2-3

Week 22 Reflection

This week, we again see the psalmist unknowingly predict the coming of Christ – and the salvation He offers us. David tells the reader that his very soul thirsts for God, much in the same way a "deer longs for streams of water." As the deer seeks water to refresh its body and give it strength, David recognizes that God provides the same for his soul. What the king describes is a feeling that I know I, and perhaps many of you, have felt on multiple occasions. It is a feeling of longing; a feeling of desire in our hearts that goes beyond this world. Our souls long for something more than what this world can offer. It is a tragic case that all too often we try to satisfy this longing with the material. We commit every sin in the pursuit of quenching our thirst. But what we find are things too small to fill our hearts and provide true satisfaction. All the while, the deceiver tries to convince us that we just need *more*. More food; more drugs; more alcohol; more parties; more entertainment; more pleasurable company.

The psalmist, however, reminds us of the truth. Only God can quench the thirst of our souls. This same reality is revealed to a Samaritan woman, when Jesus comes to visit her at the well. Thirsty, and in need of a drink, He asks the woman if she would give Him some of the water she was drawing. The woman, a great sinner, replies by telling Jesus that he shouldn't be asking such a thing. You see, the well was sacred to the Samaritans, being built by Jacob, the great patriarch. For Jesus (a Galilean man) to ask her (a Samaritan woman) for such a thing was unheard of. But Christ, for her salvation, reveals to her the truth. He says, "Everyone who drinks this water, shall be thirsty again; but whoever drinks the water I shall give will never be thirsty." (John 4:13-14) Christ reminds us all that when we chase after the things of this world, we will be left thirsty and still wanting. But if we seek Him, who is the water that gives life, our thirsts shall be quenched, and we will be satisfied.

Weekly Thoughts

Week 23

Do not fear when a man becomes rich,
when the wealth of his house grows great.
At his death he will not take along anything,
his glory will not go down after him.

Psalms 49:17-18

Week 23 Reflection

    For this week's psalm, I wish to remind the dear reader of another simple and often heard phrase: *You can't take it with you.* As sad as it might be to initially consider, it is reality that the things of this world are passing away. Every day, we see all the great testaments of our civilization being eroded by the steady hand of time. Buildings, businesses, fashion, technology, even empires and cultures; all pass away. The things that give us pleasure now will not appear in the next world. So, heed the Savior's command and "store up riches in Heaven." (Matthew 6:20) For these will be eternal riches that shall never fade or lose their luster. You will have them always.

Weekly Thoughts

Week 24

Have mercy on me, God,
for I am treated harshly;
attackers press me all the day.
My foes treat me harshly all the day;
yes, many are my attackers.
O Most High, when I am afraid,
in You I place my trust.
I praise the word of God;
I trust in God; I do not fear.

Psalms 56:2-5

Week 24 Reflection

I wish to expound upon two ideas that are present in this week's psalm. First, the idea of being surrounded by enemies. It is a sad reality that as we grow in our faith and devotion to God, there will be those who rise up against us. As we begin to show how God has worked in our lives for the better, there will be those who attack this notion. Brothers and sisters, please know this, before growing impatient or retaliating with hostility to those who treat you harshly. These foes of yours do not rise up of their own accord. Do not treat them with contempt, for their hearts have been filled with the lies of the Enemy. As God came to you, when you were an enemy of His word, so you must also go to them. Intercede on their behalf; pray that they may overcome the snares of the devil, and cast him out into the abyss. Pray for them in the name of Christ – the name above all names.

The second idea I wish to speak of is found towards the end of the psalm. It answers the question, "What do I do when I am surrounded?" What can you do? The answer is simple: Nothing. You cannot lash out in blind anger, for then, you will carry the same guilt as those who oppress you. But you alone cannot fight great multitudes; your strength will fail, and you will be overwhelmed. So, the only option left is to take the advice of the psalmist. When you are afraid, when you are oppressed, place your trust in the Lord. Praise Him Who is most trustworthy and deserving of all praise. Give all your heart – both strengths and weaknesses – and trust in His Power, Mercy, and Justice. Trust in Him, and "Do not fear."

Weekly Thoughts

Week 25

*My soul rests in God alone,
from whom comes my salvation.
God alone is my rock and salvation, my fortress;
I shall never fall.*

Psalms 62:2-3

Week 25 Reflection

    I wish to use this week's psalm as more of a reminder than a lesson. I want you to view it as you would an event written on a calendar, or an alarm set to go off on a particular date or at a particular time. We have already spoken together about envisioning God as a mighty fortress; a protection against hardship. We have gone over, in detail, how this happens and what it means for our lives. With these past lessons in mind, I want you to take the next step. I want you to pray the psalm this week. Be reminded that, because we place our trust in Him, we shall never fall.

Weekly Thoughts

Week 26

O God, you are my God – it is You I seek!
For You my body yearns;
For You my soul thirsts…

Psalms 63:2

Week 26 Reflection

The psalm this week comes to us as a direct challenge to our worldly desires. I remind you, dear reader, that it is the truth of this life that all material things shall pass away. We have already spoken about how we should not try to hold on to the riches of this world, but instead, store up riches in Heaven. Now, I ask you, when you wake up in the morning, what is your first desire? When you wake from sleep, at the start of your day, what do you wish for? When you go to bed, before you close your eyes, what are your final thoughts? My dear readers, we must strive to make our first and last thoughts a praise of God and His mercy. We must seek God with all that we are. When we wake, we must praise Him for a new day. When we go to bed, we must praise Him for the opportunities present in our lives on a daily basis. Repeat this psalm and make a change in your life. Desire God, with all your mind, body, and soul.

Weekly Thoughts

Week 27

To You we owe our hymn of praise, O God on Zion;
to You our vows must be fulfilled,
You who hears our prayers.

Psalms 65:2-3

Week 27 Reflection

Welcome, my dearest friends! You have made it to the halfway point of this book. If you have read only one psalm a week, this means that you have also made it halfway through the year. I hope that it has been a blessed year indeed, rich in God's fulfillment. I ask that you take a moment for yourselves before continuing. Pause for just a second and celebrate all that you have already accomplished. For 183 days, you have used this book to do as the first psalm instructed, meditating on the word of God, day and night. You have read, re-read, and contemplated the psalms and their accompanying reflections. You have considered how they might provide insight into your own life. Perhaps you were a believer before picking up this book and have, since reading, had your faith deepened. Maybe, more miraculously, you were not a believer, but since starting this journey with me have come to the faith.

In either case, I say rejoice! For God makes no distinction between those who are faithful. He celebrates with all the angels in Heaven over even one lost soul returning to Him. I hope that as you continue with your faith journey, this book may continue to provide you with comfort, wisdom, and support. But know this, dear brothers and sisters, that even if it has helped and continues to help, I take no credit for your deepening of faith. Indeed, the psalmist advises that my "hymn of praise" for your transformation is owed to God. It is

He, after being shown your willingness to have Him work in your life, who sent the Holy Spirit to work in your heart. So, lift up your hymns of prayer and praise to Him who is Lord of all Creation.

Weekly Thoughts

Week 28

To You all flesh must come with its burden of wicked deeds.
We are overcome by our sins; only You can pardon them.

Psalms 65:3-4

Week 28 Reflection

When you first read the psalm this week (or, indeed, when you re-read it for the second or third time) you may be, initially, disheartened. This is a truly understandable reaction. So, my dear readers, if it is yours, do not be ashamed. No one likes to be reminded of their sins. Even those who claim to not believe in the notion of sin, only choose to do so, so as not to be reminded. We do not like to be called sinners, a word that recalls in our minds our failings and misdeeds. And surely, the word "wicked" strikes us with a truly unpleasant feeling.

But, my friends, do not let sorrow grow in your hearts. If it is there, let it fade with my next words. For in this psalm, we actually find words of great encouragement and joy. King David tells us that, even though we may be "burdened of wicked deeds", we can always return to God. Even when we are "overcome by our sins", we are told that the Lord can "pardon them." This week's psalm is not one of condemnation. Instead, it is truly a song of hope.

The truth of this psalm is the truth found throughout the Bible. A truth echoed through time and spoken by many throughout the ages. No matter our burdens, no matter our sins, we are not forsaken. We are called to run to God with our burdens and lay them down at His feet. There, by the amazing gift of His salvation, we are renewed. By the sacrifice of the cross, all peoples, for all time, can be redeemed. We are never too far gone that God can't forgive us. His desire is for all His children to be with Him in Heaven. And to this end, we are called to be forgiven.

Weekly Thoughts

Week 29

May God be gracious to us and bless us;
may His face shine upon us.
So shall Your way be known upon the Earth,
Your victory among all the nations.

Psalms 67:2-3

Week 29 Reflection

Would you like to hear something amazing? Something that has often been misrepresented as a "secret", when it is, in fact, no secret at all? In actuality, what I am about to tell you has been proclaimed all over the world for the past two thousand years! Your fight against the Enemy – the battle for your very soul – is over. The war was waged, and Satan defeated. Christ stands victorious for all time, the Savior of the World. Of course, you must always stand ready to resist the devil and his temptations. You must fortify your heart and mind, so as not to give into his lies. But the ultimate victory, the one that decided your redemption, is already won.

This week, along with the usual petition for God's grace to fall upon him, the psalmist speaks to the truth of Christ's victory over sin and death. He reminds us that, just as God's grace will be known to us, so too, will His victory be made known to all of the earth. In fact, it is you, my dear readers, that are called to sing this victory to all the nations of the world. So, rejoice! For even though we are sinners, we are all chosen for this special task.

Weekly Thoughts

Week 30

*Graciously rescue me, God!
Come quickly to help me, Lord...!
Those who long for Your help always say,
"God be glorified!"*

Psalms 70:2,5

Week 30 Reflection

  For this week, my brothers and sisters, I would like you all to just reflect on a question I wish to pose to you. When you are in the depths of sorrow, do you still find the strength to glorify God? When you are crying out for Him to rescue you, do you make sure that such a request goes hand-in-hand with a praise of His mighty power to do so. Remember, dear readers, the Lord is always with you; He is ever present. Trust in his power to save you. Even in the midst of the storm, give glory and praise to Him who is faithful. Be like those the psalmist mentions. When you long for the help of God, shout to Him, "God be glorified!"

Weekly Thoughts

Week 31

*How good God is to the upright,
to those who are pure of heart!
But, as for me, my feet had almost stumbled;
my steps had nearly slipped, because I was
envious of the arrogant when I saw the
prosperity of the wicked.*

Psalms 73:1-3

Week 31 Reflection

My friends, how often we do as the psalmist has described! Is it not within our fallen nature to act as he has written? We are called to live "upright", to make our lives beautiful examples of God's everlasting mercy and kindness. Those who do not believe should be able to look at the way we live and carry ourselves, and be able to understand that we are set apart. And by this recognition, those who have strayed may be brought – by curiosity first, then by faith – to know the Creator and His will.

But we, in our human frailty, see the unjust and say, "Why do *they* prosper?" We look about us and see those who openly curse and mock God, by word and deed, live well. We are told "cheaters never prosper," and yet we see the exact opposite is often true in our societies. We grow tired with our struggles, and reason that giving in and becoming like the wicked is how we might gain for ourselves all that they have. For who doesn't wish to live in comfort; for himself and his family to prosper?

But amen, I say to you, look upon the earthly pleasures that these are given in abundance, and despair. For woe to any man who loves this life more than he loves the Lord. All these things will pass away; all that gives pleasure now will be no comfort in the grave. We who struggle in the name of God have the richer reward. Yes, it may not be your lot that you should take cruises or buy the fastest car or have the biggest house. But it is you, who has faith in the Eternal and Ever Living God, that will have the greater pleasure in Heaven. Remain "upright" my friends, and do not be jealous of those who seem to have the favor of this world. You have the favor of the Lord, your God. That is more precious than all the jewels of the earth.

Weekly Thoughts

Week 32

*I cry aloud to God; I cry to God to hear me.
On the day of my distress, I seek the LORD.*

Psalms 77:2-3

Week 32 Reflection

My absolute favorite movie series of all time also happens to be my favorite book series as well. I admit to you all, my dear friends, that I am an avid *Lord of the Rings* fan. I know the movies by heart, and make it a point to read the entire series at least once a year. It is a wonderful story, written by one of history's greatest authors, and influenced by his profound faith. I don't wish to spoil the story (for the small handful of you who have yet to see or read it), but I do want to quote to you, my dear readers, a line spoken by Gandalf (a wizard) in the last film of the trilogy. In a touching, and rather bitter-sweet moment, Gandalf says to the four hobbits gathered before him – hobbits being little people, and the four in question being our main characters – "I will not say 'do not weep', for not all tears are an evil."

This week, the psalmist comes to us with advice that can often times, for many, be difficult to follow. When life gets you down, when it has rendered you utterly helpless and you feel despair growing inside you... cry. Let your tears flow. Water is often used as a symbol of cleansing in the Bible, and tears are no different. Through tears, confess your hurt to God. For the Bible even says that God has numbered your tears. Not a single one goes unnoticed. Do not be afraid to show how vulnerable you are to the Lord. For true faith is not shown through our strength, it is shown through our weakness.

How many more would come to believe in Christ if we showed, not how strong we are, but how weak? Those who see our great strength think to themselves, 'that could never be me.' But those who see our weakness, and how we rely on God – who is true strength – will be better able to humble themselves as we have. In our shared weakness, we will find commonality. In our shared reliance on God's strength, we will forge brotherhood. So, on the day of your distress, "seek the Lord." "Cry aloud to God," who will see your tears and comfort you. Do not be afraid to cry to Him, who loves you most dearly. "For not all tears are an evil."

Weekly Thoughts

Week 33

*Because you have the LORD for your refuge
and have made the Most High your stronghold,
no evil shall befall you,
no affliction come near your tent.*

Psalms 91:9-10

Week 33 Reflection

To some, the response you may have upon reading these words is, "Amen!" To others, maybe even the majority, you may say to yourselves, "Yeah, right." Why do I predict two different responses to the same psalm? Because of what the psalm promises. It says that if we trust in God, believe in Him, "no evil shall befall" us. We read that, by making God our stronghold, "no affliction" will "come near."

The reader who says, "Amen", does so because times have been good to them. They got the promotion. They got the job. They got the car. They got a date. They praise the Lord because they perceive His favor in their life, if only through material gain. Those who read this psalm and scoff, do so because life has been rough as of late – or even for quite some time. They got passed over for the promotion. The company wouldn't hire them. The car broke down. They got rejected or dumped. They scoff because they don't see God providing all these things. They may even blame Him for taking things away.

To those who have such reactions, I have a question for you. Would you feel the same way if the roles were reversed? If things went poorly, would those who were rejoicing now curse God? If things finally started going right, would those who cursed Him now praise His name? It is easy to praise when things are well, and easy to doubt when things are not well. But if either case is true, then those who have such opinions do not know the true God. Those who only bless because they receive blessings, have a limited understanding of the true nature of the Almighty. The faith they have is one of convenience, where, as long as God keeps providing goodness, they will praise His name.

But you might be now saying to yourselves, "Well then, how can the psalm be true if I praise God and yet still have tragedy in my life?" Firstly, because God is neither the source nor the cause of such tragedies. God wants only good things for us. He has a plan for our lives, a plan with Him included, that will see us navigating the difficult waters of our world and living well. It is only when we chose to stray from this plan, to go our own way, that we find ourselves experiencing hardship. The Enemy exists in our world for such times as this, throwing pain your way to make you doubt God and lose faith in Him. But do not be discouraged. For even though God is not the source of this pain, He can still use it for your benefit. He can use such times of trial to get you back on track.

Secondly, the psalm itself does not directly mention worldly afflictions – though God can help with those too. Trusting in God does not inherently mean that the car will suddenly become undamaged or our boss will have a change of heart and give us that promotion. Instead, trusting in God will, first and foremost, help us spiritually. You may not end up going on the date with the person you wanted, but take heart. God will give you the strength to wait. He has in mind a person for you; if you trust Him, he will send them your way. And, if it is not God's will that you should marry, He will help you to understand why. "Trust" does not mean "transaction". We are not buying gifts from God using trust as the currency. Instead, we are learning to grow in spirit. The afflictions that won't come near us are spiritual ones. The tent is your heart, and by making God your fortress, it will be protected.

Weekly Thoughts

Week 34

*It is good to give thanks to the LORD,
to sing praise to Your name, Most High,
to proclaim Your love at daybreak,
Your faithfulness in the night.*

Psalms 92:2-3

Week 34 Reflection

When you first began reading this book, my brothers and sisters, I told you about how following God is not something that can be mastered in a single day. Instead, it requires us to meditate on His word, "day and night." It is a daily task we have, to come to know the Lord and to do His will. A task that, I myself, sometimes struggle with. But by following the advice of the psalmist, and coming to realize that this journey in faith is a life-long one, I find myself able to do what God has asked of me. And so, you will also.

Here, now, the psalm this week offers us another practice for us to keep. One that will help us as we travel the path of salvation. A path, both easily strayed from and easily found again, thanks to the Lord. After your meditation, however long it takes, do what the psalmist advises. Give praise to God. Say a simple, "Thank you", both for what He has revealed to you and for what He chooses to keep hidden. For both serve a purpose, known only to God. When the day begins, proclaim His great love. When the night comes, proclaim His great faithfulness.

Weekly Thoughts

Week 35

*Sing to the LORD a new song;
sing to the LORD all the Earth.
Sing to the LORD, bless His name;
proclaim His salvation day after day.
Tell His glory among the nations;
among all peoples His marvelous deeds.*

Psalms 96:1-3

Week 35 Reflection

Roman occupied Palestine; the southern province, known as Judea. It is approximately two thousand years ago, around 34 AD. A new religion is born in the heart of the Jewish nation – the city of Jerusalem. This new faith, called "The Way" by the Romans, will accomplish what no other had managed before. In the past, when one nation conquered another, the people of the conquered region were assimilated into the dominant nation's culture. Though Babylon was their homeland, the peoples living there were made Persian citizens when Cyrus the Great took control of the area. Under this new rule, the people spoke the language, learned how to navigate the economy, and took on the religious aspects of their rulers. Most even converted to the official religion of the empire. So it was, when Greece conquered Persia and Rome conquered Greece.

But now, a new religion was about to break that cycle. It didn't ask that its followers give up their nationality. Aside from a few specific vices, it didn't even ask them to give up their way of life. It didn't emphasize a strict adherence to a set of laws, and was not the religion of the empire that ruled most of the world at the time. Miraculously, however, this new religion would show that it could cross city, state, province, and even territorial lines. It managed to break barriers of speech and nationality, and was spreading like wildfire all over the Mediterranean. It called into fellowship all manner of people, from all walks of life. Rich and poor; slave and free; Jew and Greek; old and young; educated and not. All were called to be a part of this new movement. From Jerusalem, to the rest of Judea and Samaria, then outwards to every nation in the Roman Empire. People in Damascus, Antioch, Philippi, Corinth, even the great cities of Athens and Rome heard the call. The first in this faith, called Apostles, were on a mission. Spread the Good News "to the ends of the Earth." (Acts 1:8)

Now, fast forward almost a full two millennium. The year is now 2004. A man, named Christopher Tin, composes a song titled "Baba Yetu" to be used as the main theme of the computer game *Civilization IV*. When the game is released in October, 2005, it gains instant acclaim, as does its beautiful main track. Six years pass, with the game becoming internationally known, as well as internationally successful. Then, at the 2011 Grammy Awards ceremony, "Baba Yetu" wins the Grammy for Best Arrangement, Instrumentals, and Vocals. It marks a milestone in the industry, as the song becomes the first ever composed for a video game to win a major award. Because of the win, the song itself becomes as well known as the game it was created for. But as exciting as this story is, you may well be wondering how it ties into the origin of the Christian faith. Or how either relates to this week's psalm.

We have been told in previous weeks to bring our praises to the Lord. We have been told to sing and dance before Him, for it is good. The Lord rejoices with us, and delights in our merriment. This week's psalm is no different, as we start off by reading, "Sing to the Lord a new song." But the psalm continues. It tells us that, through our song of praise, we should sing to all the earth. Through our song, we should be praising God before others. The psalmist writes that we, much like the Apostles, should "Tell His glory among the nations." He recognizes that the glory of God should be sung by everyone, everywhere. By all peoples, of all nations. Every tongue that speaks should sing the praise of the Lord. In every language, we should hear the people rejoice for God.

This was the mission of the Apostles. Handed down to them by Christ himself. It was Christ's hope that all would be called to Him, and that all would share in the goodness of God. For this reason, the Apostles were told to, "Go therefore and make disciples of all nations." (Matthew 28:19) They gave everything they had, including their own lives, to the fulfillment of this commission. Now, here we stand, with evidence of their great work. Christopher Tin's song is a fruit of their labor, their sacrifice. For, the Swahili "Baba Yetu" translates in English as "Our Father". This song, recognized all over the world and sung by just as many, is simply the Lord's Prayer. And it is being sung "among all peoples."

Weekly Thoughts

Week 36

*The LORD is king; let the Earth rejoice…
justice and right are the foundation of His throne.*

Psalms 97:1,2

Week 36 Reflection

The psalm for this week comes to remind us of two very important things. Firstly, that God is King. Not *a* king or *some* king, but *the* King. He alone is Lord of Creation, the First and the Last. This fact is perfectly summed up in His most holy name. In the book of Exodus, when Moses is led to the burning bush and has an experience of God (a theophany), he asks God for His name. That way, when he returns to lead the Hebrews out of slavery in Egypt, Moses will be able to tell them who sent him. God responds thusly: "I Am who I Am… this is what you will tell the Israelites: I Am has sent me to you." (Exodus 3:14) God's very being is defined by existence. He *was not* or *will be*, but *is*. For Him, there is no past or future, but only the present. For in Him, all things *are*. He *is* King Eternal.

Secondly, the psalm reminds us that the very essence of His holy kingship is "justice and right". These two aspects of God's nature, awesome and mysterious, are the "foundation of His throne." God does not rule us for the things we provide Him, for there is nothing made by human hands that He desires. He needs neither our works nor our praise to exist. For He *was* before all things *were*. He does not rule because he desires land or their riches. He does not seek new land for exploration or plunder. Instead, He rules for our benefit. He is over us as Our King, because He desires fairness and mercy to be shown to us. So, take comfort, for God is the Good

King. He rules with love and compassion. Of us, his subjects, He desires only our hearts; to love Him as much as He loves us.

Weekly Thoughts

Week 37

*The LORD has made His victory known;
has revealed His triumph
in the sight of the nations.*

Psalms 98:2

Week 37 Reflection

The victory of the Lord is made known when we look upon the cross. It is revealed in its entirety when we behold the crucified Son of God. He who was put to death to pay the debt of humanity, and thus rescue us from the fiery pit. By Christ's death, death itself no longer holds sway over us. Our sins are forgiven, and the way to Heaven paved before us. Wherever there are believers of Jesus, this ultimate victory is proclaimed. Let us not be afraid to praise this victory "in the sight of the nations."

Weekly Thoughts

Week 38

*Know that the LORD is God,
He made us; we belong to Him.*

Psalms 100:3

Week 38 Reflection

How many times, in our lives, have we felt like we do not belong? I confess, my brothers and sisters, that this was something that I struggled with for a long time. I considered myself an outlier, too different from everyone else to fully share all that I am with anyone. And nothing set me more apart from others than my faith in God. Maybe, when you were younger, you didn't feel like you quite fit in with your group of friends. Maybe you still don't. Maybe you felt like you were on your own at work, school, or even church – the one place we should feel welcome, part of a community.

But, my dear friends, I ask you: why do you chase the approval of mortal men? Yes, it is good to cultivate friendships and to live in peace with your fellow man. But the truth is there is only one to whom you truly belong... God. You were handcrafted by the Almighty, fearfully and wonderfully made. There is not a single human being on this planet quite like you, and that's the way He likes it. Before the foundation of the universe, God had already decided this world would be better if it had you in it. In fact, God loved you so much, He decided that He would rather die, than risk spending an eternity without you. Your salvation is a product of God's fondness of you. We tend to look upon the cross and see what was done for humanity as a whole. But now, I urge you, look upon the cross and say, "That was done for *me*."

If you feel left out, like you don't quite "fit in", don't worry. The truth is, neither did Jesus. Even in His own hometown, the people treated Our Lord harshly. He preached to them change; salvation through faith, grace for all, and peace before war. Thankfully, Jesus never let the harsh words of others embitter His spirit. He took comfort in the knowledge that all of us belong to God, first and foremost. None can love us as much as He, who is Father to all. It is in His arms we find where we truly belong.

Weekly Thoughts

Week 39

Bless the LORD, my soul;
all my being, bless His holy name!
Bless the LORD, my soul... Who pardons all your sins,
and heals all your ills,
who redeems your life from the Pit.

Psalms 103:1-4

Week 39 Reflection

"Bless the Lord, oh my soul, oh my soul! Worship His holy name!" These words – almost exactly the same as those of the psalm – are found in the song "Ten Thousand Reasons". The focus of the song, written and performed by Matt Redman, is to praise God for all the good He does in our lives. While there may not be *exactly* ten thousand reasons listed in either the song or this week's psalm (if there were, it would probably make either the longest of its kind) the writer does provide some specific examples of God's grace.

First, He "pardons all your sins." We are encouraged to bring all of our doubts, worries, faults, and personal weaknesses to the Lord. Above all, we are called to confess our sins to Him. We lay them all down before Him. There, at the foot of the cross, we find our forgiveness. Second, we are told that, through this awe-inspiring forgiveness, we are healed of "all your ills." This means that Christ is ready to heal us, both inside and out. Starting with our broken spirits, we are fixed – put back together by the grace of God.

Finally (and perhaps, chiefly) we are told that the Lord "redeems your life from the Pit." Of all the reasons to praise God, this should be at the top of our lists. Here, we are reminded – by both song and psalm – that not even the powers of hell can hold us. They cannot stand against the power and mercy of the Lord. By the grace of God, and the love of Christ, we can all be rescued. The Pit, much like the grave, can no longer chain us. We are free. For these reasons, "Bless the Lord, oh my soul, oh my soul!" Let us all worship His holy name.

Weekly Thoughts

Week 40

Some had lost their way in a barren desert;
found no path toward a city to live in.
They were hungry and thirsty;
their life was ebbing away.
In their distress they cried to the LORD,
who rescued them in their peril,
guided them by a direct path,
so they reached a city to live in.

Psalms 107:4-7

Week 40 Reflection

This week's psalm calls us to remember all the times God has rescued us from peril. It invites us to reflect on the consistency with which He comes to us when we cry out in need. The writer uses Psalm 107 to do some reflecting of his own, calling forth the history of the nation of Israel. A history that found the nation and its people in a deeply personal relationship with God.

The "barren desert" is easily understood to be a reference to the wilderness of the Sinai Peninsula, which the ancient Hebrew people wandered in after their flight from Egypt. After disobeying God, the Israelites were forced into a nomadic lifestyle for forty years; instead of returning to their homeland of Canaan, they had "lost their way" in the wilderness." They "found no path toward a city to live in", simply rambling until they had learned to fully trust in the Lord. When they had, God came to them and gave them strength enough to retake their homeland. He "guided them by a direct path" to the place they belonged. There, He would provide them with "a city to live in."

Our own lives can often feel like the desert that the Israelites wandered in. It can be a long, grueling, uncomfortable experience. We often feel as if our reality is defined by barrenness and hardship. Also – much like the Hebrew people did during their wandering – we tend to bring, not our praises, but our complaints to God. We complain to Him about our misery and suffering, as if it were His will for us to suffer so. We are called to lay our burdens before Him, and accept His mercy, counsel, and compassion. Instead, we bring our grievances and blame, expecting only the firm hand of a strict ruler. We claim God himself is the author of our suffering!

How foolish we humans can be. For if we look to the story which the psalmist is referencing, we will see the truth. When the Israelites arrived at the edge of the Promised Land, twelve spies were chosen (one from each tribe) to determine the military strength of those who dwelled in the region. While two – Joshua and Caleb – trusted in the Lord's word that they would overcome their foes, the other ten men disagreed. So, they brought back a sour report to Moses and Aaron, saying it was impossible to retake their homeland. Even though God had promised the land to them, they doubted His promise and despaired. It was for *this* reason that they wandered in the desert. Not because God was angry and sought to punish, but because the Israelites needed to learn the lesson that many of us still need reminding of. Trust in God. Through Him, all things are possible.

Even after such disobedience, God loves us still. He still seeks to help us on our faith journeys, for the destination is worth the hardship. The moment we begin to trust in the Lord, Our God, is the moment we are led out of the desert. Like the Magi, who followed the star to the Christ child, we are led by *the* Light out of our darkness. This does not mean trouble will never come; it is a fact of this world that it will. The Enemy always seeks to blind us to the Truth using our pain and hardship. But to trust that God will lead us is also to trust that He will be with us in such trying times. When we stumble and fall, as long as we do not lose sight of Him, the Lord will pick us up. He will help us to endure the deserts of this life, until we find rest and comfort in the city He is leading us to. The Eternal City of God.

Weekly Thoughts

Week 41

*I will praise the LORD with all my heart
in the assembled congregation of the upright.
Great are the works of the LORD,
studied by all you delight in them.
Majestic and glorious is His works.*

Psalms 111:1-3

Week 41 Reflection

It is not a bad thing to have some time alone with God. Just you, Him, and a quiet space. In fact, in the Gospels, Jesus actually recommends that it is better to pray in secret. He says that, instead of shouting and boasting of your faith on street corners, it is better for you to make your faith deeply personal. Make it something only you and your Father in Heaven will know about. The Apostle Paul also says that faith in Christ is not something to boast about, like you would boast about getting a promotion.

However, we human beings are made to live in community. Not just *a* community, surrounded by others but never talking or getting to know them, but *in* community; to truly love our neighbors as ourselves. To share in as much of their lives as we can, and to share with them in the life of Christ. The psalmist this week reminds us to not neglect our spiritual community. He advises us to get together and praise the Lord with one voice; to praise Him as a "congregation of the upright."

Weekly Thoughts

Week 42

*Blessed the man who fears the LORD,
who greatly delights in His commands…
The wicked sees and is angry,
gnashes his teeth and wastes away;
The desire of the wicked comes to nothing.*

Psalms 112:1,10

Week 42 Reflection

The world we live in today is much unlike what it was a hundred years ago. As the faithful of Christ, it seems as if there exist foes around every corner. We are reminded through movies, music, tv shows, and even news programs that belief in Christ is not the norm. Despite the fact that a majority of the world believes in God, we are made to feel by those in charge as if the world is against us. The name of God is slandered, and those who trust in His commands are ridiculed and made to feel shame.

But I say to you, brothers and sisters, do not be afraid to express your love of God. For He has great love for you. There will be those who curse you, this I do not deny. There will be those, deceived by the Enemy, that do not believe in God or His judgement or His mercy. Because of your belief, they will use every way possible to hurt you. But take heart, for the psalmist says that "the wicked… wastes away." All that is evil in this world is passing, preparing the way for the coming of the Lord. And when Christ comes in victory, the wicked shall see the folly of their ways. All they hold dear will be ground into dust and thrown into the Pit. But we, the faithful of God, shall rejoice with God in Heaven.

Weekly Thoughts

Week 43

*Not to us, not to us but to Your name give glory
because of Your mercy and faithfulness...
Their idols are silver and gold, the work of human hands...
Their makers will be like them, and anyone who trusts in them.*

Psalms 115:1,4,8

Week 43 Reflection

I must confess to you, my dear readers, that when I look at today's society I weep. I look around and see a people misguided and being led from God. I ask you: what do we exalt? People these days concern themselves too much with things of "silver and gold" – things that have material value. The psalm references a time not unlike our own. After the reign of King Solomon, who had grown apart from the God of his father David, the nation of Israel was divided in two. Of the twelve tribes, 10 made their home in the north. They called themselves Israel and had Samaria as the capital city. The other two tribes made up the southern kingdom, Judah, with its capital of Jerusalem. A line of kings was instituted to rule each nation. While some rulers were good of heart and feared the Lord, most spurned His kindness and worshipped false gods.

The psalm speaks to how both nations were less than faithful to the One, True God. Instead of giving praise to Him, the people of Judah and Israel worshipped man-made idols. Brothers and sisters, is this not a description of our present times? We exalt diets for their ability to change our bodies. We exalt fashion designers for their clothes. We exalt sports stars for their athleticism; riots have started over a team winning or losing a big game. We exalt politicians, handing over to them every kind of freedom. What were gifts from

God, we give to men and women who deem themselves "better" and "more qualified".

We exalt *ourselves*, dear friends – our art, entertainment, science, technology, architecture. Instead of beautiful murals of Christ's life, friends, and mission, we splash paint on a bare canvas and call it "divine". Instead of making movies that depict epic battles of good versus evil, with good triumphing, we depict every sort of grotesque imagery. Movies and television now make us angry or sad. Our heroes no longer speak to the true goodness of mankind, but instead offer reflections of our deepest flaws. Science and technology have been perverted, no longer being for the advancement of human knowledge, but being for the advancement of human exaltation. What great men once used to prove the Creator, we now use in a vain attempt to deny His existence. Like those who built the Tower of Babel, we make buildings, ugly in design, only to stand as monuments to human achievement.

This is all completely backwards to how we are called to live. You know it, I know it, and the psalmist knew it. It is God, and the Trinity, that should be exalted. If a doctor cures a patient, it is only by the talents that God gave him that he does so. If an athlete wins the top prize, it is because he followed the Bible teaching of treating his body like a temple, and was thus able to maximize all that God put in him. All human achievement – from a painting to a scientific breakthrough – should glorify the name of the Lord. "Not to us", but to the One who made all things, yet loves *us* beyond all things, should all praise be given.

Weekly Thoughts

Week 44

*For my soul has been freed from death,
my eyes from tears, my feet from stumbling.
I shall walk before the LORD
in the land of the living.*

Psalms 116:8-9

Week 44 Reflection

This week the psalmist, through the divine hand of God's will, has once again foretold of the coming Messiah, Jesus. He speaks to the salvation that will (from his point of view) be given to all when the Lord comes in glory. A salvation poured out for all mankind. A wholly unique salvation, as it will be offered directly from the hand of God; freely given, for all who wish to receive it.

In both the Christian and Jewish faiths – as well as many faiths that now populate the globe – there exists a bicameral view of the afterlife. There is a "land of the living" and a "land of the dead"; a Heaven and a hell. While some Christian faiths believe in a third option (traditional Catholicism believes in a place called Purgatory) these two primary realms are a shared belief by the two religions, as well as many others. The "land of the dead" has had many names over the course of human history. Hell, Tartarus, Hades, Sheol, Gehenna; all monikers for this place of darkness. It is a place, as Christ Himself describes it, filled with the sound of "weeping and gnashing of teeth." A fiery furnace of torment and pain.

But do not despair, my dear readers. For the psalmist comes to us with good news. In fact, though he did not realize it, he came with *the* Good News. From this land of the dead, our souls have been freed. The penalty of death eternal has been paid for by the sacrifice of Christ on the cross. What was once promised to us by Adam – that being assured destruction – was now undone by God. As all men once died because of the Original Sin, now all live because Christ has become sin for us. He has borne our punishment, descending into hell and then rising into Heaven. There, He is seated at the right hand of the Father. By trusting in Him, the grave no longer frightens us. Death has lost its sting.

But now we ask, "where is this land of the living?" Surely, it is not here on earth. Truly, I tell you, do not look for it among the riches of this life. For though we have created all manner of things to give pleasure, they are fleeting in nature, and shall pass away. Because of this, we tend to fall into despair. "Why would God rescue us from hell, if our only reward is this life on earth? A life that is filled with struggle and trial after trial. How can this be our reward if we still grow weak and die? How can this be the land of the living, if there is still death?" It is because the *true* land of the living is in a place that will not pass away. A place that is eternal because the One who made it is eternal. My brothers and sisters, as followers of Christ we do not hope for things in this life. Instead, we hope for the life everlasting that awaits us in Heaven. There, our souls truly live, rescued by God. It is there, that we "shall walk before the Lord in the land of the living."

Weekly Thoughts

Week 45

How can the young keep his way without fault?
Only by observing Your words.
With all my heart I seek You;
Do not let me stray from Your commandments.

Psalms 119:9-10

Week 45 Reflection

There is a reality we must all face, my brothers and sisters. Browse the internet and you'll find dozens of websites designed to attract children. Stroll the isles of a book store and you'll find numerous books on parenting. Sit in on a "health science" class – offered to younger and younger age groups – and be horrified as the state teaches children about their bodies. It seems in today's society the only people not parenting children... are parents.

Put away the self-help books. Turn off the television, usually only on to distract us for some time. Instead, grab a Bible and listen to the psalm. The writer assures us that the foundation of a child's life – and the foundation of *our* lives as adults – should be to not "stray from [God's] commandments." If this sounds like a daunting task, do not fret. For Christ has simplified it for us. The Israelites, once given the Ten Commandments, wanted to make sure there was a law, based on these commandments, for every conceivable instance of life. When Jesus was born, the Hebrew people had concocted some 600 individual laws. For us, who follow Christ, we need only two.

We are called to follow two simple commands. We are to love God, with all our hearts, all our minds, all our bodies, all our souls, and to love our neighbors as ourselves. By claiming the faith of Christ, we become observers of God's commands, just as He was. But Jesus promised that His burden was light. By following these two *new* commandments – perfections of the Ten – we build for ourselves a strong foundation for our lives. A foundation that, if built early in our lives, will serve us well throughout our days.

Weekly Thoughts

Week 46

*Those who sow in tears will reap with shouts of joy.
Those who go forth weeping, carrying sacks of seed,
will return with cries of joy, carrying their bundled sheaves.*

Psalms 126:5-6

Week 46 Reflection

*Blessed are they who mourn, for they will be comforted...
Blessed are they who hunger and thirst for righteousness,
for they will be satisfied...
Blessed are they who are persecuted for the sake of righteousness,
for theirs is the Kingdom of Heaven.*

Matthew 5:4,6,10

Thank you, Lord, for you assure me that my sorrow shall pass. My tears pave the way to Heaven.

Weekly Thoughts

Week 47

Out of the depths I call to You, LORD; LORD hear my cry!
May You be attentive to my cry for mercy.
If You, LORD, keep account of sins, LORD, who can stand?
But with You is forgiveness and so You are revered.

Psalms 130:1-4

Week 47 Reflection

How wonderful the psalmist's words this week! They speak to the truth of God's very nature. While we can never comprehend it fully, we can marvel at what has been revealed to us. We can behold the heart of the Lord.

In every faith on this planet – barring faith in and of Christ – there exists no redemptive forgiveness. There is servile forgiveness only. A forgiveness by the supreme deity contingent on strict adherence to a prescribed set of rules, ministered by chosen agents on Earth. In other words, if we sin, we do so by breaking the law; if we are forgiven, we are by following the law. The law both condemns and offers recompense for redemption through ritual sacrifice and cleansing. But the law forever keeps track of our offenses, and though we may be forgiven in this life, we will face a final atonement in the next.

Not so with God, and the true faith that comes through His Son, Jesus. In this faith, you are forgiven before you even sin. God sees the choices you can and will make. And despite whatever grave mistakes you may commit, the price for such disobedience has already been paid. God does not need your offerings. He does not require lengthy prayers or good deeds done out of fear for the fire of hell. He seeks only your humble repentance; He seeks your broken heart, so that He may heal it. Like the Prodigal Son, if we stray from the righteous path of the Father, we need only to stumble a little ways back to Him before He runs to greet us.

The Lord is waiting, eagerly, for our return. The psalmist says that, if the Lord kept an account of all the sins we've committed, we would never be able to seek forgiveness. But Our Father in Heaven is Love, in its purest form. As such, the Apostle Paul states, quite clearly, God will "bear all things, believe[s] all things, hope[s] all things, endure[s] all things." He is forgiveness eternal, offered freely on the cross, to every wayward sinner.

Weekly Thoughts

Week 48

*I do not busy myself with great matters,
with things too sublime for me.
Rather, I have stilled my soul,
like a weaned child to its mother, weaned is my soul.
Israel, hope in the LORD, now and forever.*

Psalms 131:1-3

Week 48 Reflection

Let me ask you this, dear readers: how much do you concern yourselves with? How many things do you think about, or even lose sleep over? I know there are many troubling things in this world. There are wars being waged, slavery still being practiced, governments abusing their power, and all manner of obscenities being marketed to younger and younger audiences through entertainment media. On top of all this, there's your bills to worry about; your kids, family, health, job, cleaning your house, and cooking your meals. There seems to be a never-ending pile of concerns on our plates.

While it is true, there *is* much that deserves our attention, there is also equally as much that doesn't. So, the psalmist comes to us this week to remind us to lighten our load a bit. Deposit your burdens at the foot of the cross, giving all your worries to God. Does this mean we should blindly follow our government leaders? No, but we should be good citizens. Outside of doing that, we ask for God's help in all political matters. Should we not pay our bills because even looking at them is too stressful? No, but we shouldn't see money as the benchmark for happiness. Ask God for His wisdom when it comes to your finances.

I do not ask you, brothers and sisters, to be ignorant, unwise, or foolish. I am not asking you to ignore your problems; that's what those who belong to this world will try to get you to do. They say, "Don't worry about how little money you have. Buy this new fun thing, or drink, or drug, and you'll feel too good to care." Instead, when life becomes overwhelming, go to God with your burdens. When a big decision needs to be made, go to God for His counsel. Give to God everything too big for you to handle, and let Him help carry the weight of your worries.

Weekly Thoughts

Week 49

*O come, bless the LORD, all you servants of the LORD,
you who stand in the house of the LORD throughout the nights.
Lift up your hands toward the sanctuary, and bless the LORD.*

Psalms 134:1-2

Week 49 Reflection

There remain only a few weeks left in the year, and thus, only a few more entries. Our time together is ending soon, coming ever closer with every turning page. Do not think, however, that the final page of this book marks the final page of my writings. On the contrary, I plan to write to you, my dear friends, as long as my hand can grip a pen and my eyes can see a page. These last few psalms will, for now, be my last opportunities to use the words of the psalmist to impart some wisdom to you, the reader.

This week, we read, primarily, about vigilance. The psalm concerns the diligence with which we are to carry out our duty of keeping watch "throughout the nights." This phrase has two areas of relevance for our lives. Firstly, we find dark nights – and even dark days – in our day-to-day lives. By existing in this world, we experience the trials that come along with its fallen nature. The devil ever seeks to tempt us to turn from the Lord, to weaken us through the success of the wicked or the failings of the righteous. Like good soldiers, watching over the ramparts for enemies sneaking in the night, we must be ever ready to resist the sweet words of *the* Enemy.

The second area of relevance also concerns our watchfulness in this world, but on a much larger scale. As we stand at the ready to resist the devil, who holds sway over this world, we must also stand ready to greet our Lord for when He returns. Then, the earth will be made new, the devils cast into the Pit, and the faithful given glory in Heaven. We are told by Christ that the glory of God will come when we least expect it, like a thief in the night. We are told that no man will know the hour of the coming of the Lord. So, we must always have praises on our lips, and be ever ready to forgive others as we have been forgiven. For when the Lord comes, if we hold contempt in our hearts, we will not be allowed in the place He has made for us.

The psalm reminds us to be ever ready to defend the faith from the machinations of the Evil One. It reminds us to be ever ready to greet the Lord with hymns of praise and honor. We must live, every day, like it is the last one we get. In doing this, we stand vigilant, even in the dark of the night.

Weekly Thoughts

Week 50

LORD, You have probed me, you know me...
You understand my thoughts from afar...
Even before a word is on my tongue, LORD,
You know it all...
Where can I go from Your spirit?
From Your presence, where can I flee?

Psalms 139:1-2,4,7

Week 50 Reflection

I was once taught a very valuable lesson about the nature of the Bible. A lesson that has, thus far, lasted me all my life. I learned it from a video lecture series, specifically geared toward teenagers, about the Bible. It's story, it's history, and its revelations. Though the series *is* titled *The Teen Timeline*, I believe that even adult parishioners can benefit from this lighthearted, yet often profound, in-depth look at the book that has literally shaped the course of human history for the past two thousand years.

The first time I saw the series in its entirety, was when I was about 14 years old. I was in Youth Group at my church, settling into a bean-bag chair for what I could tell would be a special class. I have since re-watched the entire series (in and out of bean-bags) many times ever since. The presenter – Mark Hart – imparted, in one part of the series, the lesson I now pass on to you. The lesson is this: the true nature of the Bible is *not* a story of humanity pursuing God, but of God pursuing humanity.

We find this very sentiment being echoed in this week's psalm. It speaks first of how well God knows us. People know us as far as they know our past actions, and then judge what our future actions will most likely be. People can know our taste in music, food, art, and even our favorite color. It is only God who knows our actions before we do. It is only God who forgives our mistakes before we make them. It is only God who knows *why* a song means so much to us, or what memories of yesteryear are brought forth in our minds by eating a certain dish. He knows us more completely than any human ever can. All our thoughts, our strengths, our weaknesses, are known to Him.

Even when we are ashamed, turning from God, we are never out of His sight. Even when we say, "He cannot possibly love me", we find the opposite is true when we behold the cross. There, we see that God loves us so much, as to give Himself completely for us. No matter where we go, no matter how far or fast we run, God will be waiting at the destination to meet us. Truly, "Where can I go from Your spirit?"

Weekly Thoughts

Week 51

Great is the LORD and worthy of much praise,
Whose grandeur is beyond understanding.

Psalms 145:3

Week 51 Reflection

The psalmist this week comes to remind us of an aspect of our relationship with God. We are called to live in communion with Him. We were made to love and be loved by the Lord. Our very existence is founded on the reality that we were created to be objects of the Lord's affection. The mystery of this love – how the One, who is Perfection and Goodness, could die to save the many, who are imperfect and sinful – is at the very core of our being. It is why our hearts cry out for something more than this world can provide for us. And this mystery is not one to be *solved*, as one solves a puzzle or complex equation. It is a mystery to *behold*, embodied in its entirety on the cross.

Weekly Thoughts

Week 52

Praise God in His holy sanctuary;
give praise in the mighty dome of heaven...
Give praise with blasts upon the horn,
praise Him with harp and lyre.
Give praise with tambourines and dance,
praise Him with strings and pipes...
Let everything that has breath give praise to the LORD!

Psalms 150:1,3-4,6

Week 52 Reflection

Fitting, don't you think, that the last psalm of this book should be this one? The psalm for Week 1 was Psalm 1, and now, the final psalm for one writing shall be the final psalm of another. Also, quite fitting are the words on which we leave each other – at least, for now.

With my narrative "last breath", we come together in fulfillment of the psalm: "Let everything that has breath give praise to the Lord!" For this one last time, we speak, and are reminded of, the end result of our journey in faith. We are, all of us, called to live righteously. We are called to live in peace with our neighbor, and follow all that God has commanded. But above all these, we are called to love Him and live in love *with* Him.

The best way to show our love for the Lord is to rejoice in His name. We the faithful are called to be lights to the world, so that those who dwell in darkness may, by our stewardship, be led to He who is the True Light. To this end, we must rejoice in the name of the Lord. Sing loud and proud; let all see you delight in His name.

Pay no heed to those who say we look foolish. Recall Psalm 14 from Week 7, that assures us it is the truly foolish who do not worship the Lord. We also pray, that by such foolish dancing, others may be moved by our joy to believe in Christ.

If some say to you, "You should not be celebrating, because there is no holiday." Say in reply to them, with all kindness, "What more cause do I need to celebrate, other than to give thanks to the Lord?" If some approach you and say, "You look foolish," say in reply, "Then I am a fool for the Lord, who vindicates me." So, make merry, and do not concern yourselves with the jests of men. For, as men are lesser than God, the sneers of men are lesser than the love of God. And while they who mock continue to be separated from the Lord, rejoicing in the things of this world, we will rejoice in He who is above the world.

I, again, remind you my brothers and sisters, that this world is passing away. Those who store up riches here on earth, shall be left poor as a beggar when the Kingdom of God comes. All idols of silver and gold shall crumble to dust and be scattered with the wind. All those who rejoice now in their own might, in these idols built by their own hands, shall pass away like the things they worship. But we, who "Give praise with blasts upon the horn, praise Him with harp and lyre", shall remain with God. We, who "Give praise with tambourines and dance, praise Him with strings and pipes…", shall rejoice forever in Heaven.

The end result of our faith journey is the praise of the Father. To give to Him all glory and honor. To love Him with all of our hearts, all of our minds, all of our bodies, all of our souls. To sing praise to Him who loves us completely, both in this life and the next. As the gold and silver fades into dust, taking all who worship them to the grave, we who live in Christ shall live forever. Because we believe in Him who is the eternal Word of God – God, Himself, who came to redeem us sinners. As Christ rose on the third day in glory, so shall we, who love Him who first loved us, also rise. So, with all the angels and saints of Heaven, let us lift up our voices and our hands, exclaiming as the faithful:

Hallelujah!
Praise the LORD my soul…
The LORD shall reign forever… through all generations!
Hallelujah!

Psalms 146:1-2,10

Weekly Thoughts

Resources

"A Quote by Abraham Lincoln." *Goodreads,*
    www.goodreads.com/quotes/131220-i-can-see-how-it-might-be-possible-for-a.

Hart, Mark. *The Teen Timeline,* July 2006

The Legend of Bagger Vance. Dir. Robert Redford
    DreamWorks Pictures, 2000. Film

The Lord of the Rings: The Return of the King. Dir. Peter
    Jackson New Line Cinema, 2003. Film

The New American Bible. St. Joseph Edition ed.,
    Catholic Book Publishing Corp., 1986

The Shack. Dir. Stuart Hazeldine
    Gil Netter Productions, Windblown Media, 2017. Film

Made in the USA
Middletown, DE
08 August 2023